...garb yourself in the patience of intense creativity. Listen to the wild thoughts that are there. Listen to the wild thoughts bringing us home.

~ Joanna Macy

Dreamfruit

Lunar Tales

for earthlings

an ecopunk story and mini-journal

2026

elizabeth russell

EARTH
DRAGON
PRESS

Dreamfruit 2026: Lunar Tales for Earthlings

Copyright © 2025 by Elizabeth Russell
www.elizabethrussell.space

Cover design by Carla Alpert

Book design and layout by Ted Owen

Illustrations by Beth Lorio

Printed in the United States of America.

ISBN: 979-8-9987540-1-2

Earth Dragon Press
Eugene, Oregon

2025

You hold in your hands a kaleidoscopic map of an emerging world. Allow yourself to enter and move through these thirteen dreams as if through a storied landscape, one that pulses with its own cultural norms, characters, and magics.

Woven together, these dreams reveal a mythic map of a single and decisive year on planet Earth. They point to themes for each lunar cycle in 2026, creating a narrative of transformation in both the personal and shared realms, and a return to radical belonging within the circle of life.

Read these monthly tales as missives from our grandmother Moon or as a collective dreamstory to help you conceive a regenerative path through the changing terrain of this pivotal Earth moment.

The Dreamfruit adventure is designed to frame your personal journey within the context of the wider world. The journey is an ecospiritual one, written to enliven your vision of a viable and thriving Earth. ❧

Earthling 101

As our story begins, the living Earth has been imperiled and our creative nature is rising up.

Remember! We are earthlings-in-training. The Dreamfruit mission is to return to radical belonging. Conscious connection with the living Earth is the natural state of earthlings, but in the rush and pressures of modernity the ecological self can get left behind. Here are three key pathways to help you plot your course.

Magical Animism

Seeing the world around you as sentient will awaken your empathy and soften the distinctions between you and "other." Plants, stones, creatures, and even the written word can sparkle with mutual presence and agency.

Natural Time

Moving your mind out of linear time and into the flow of lunar cycles takes practice, but it is a surefire path to tuning into the larger cosmic intelligence. Inner states can synchronize with outer rhythms as we open to subtle cues from nature.

Deep Imagination

Symbols and dreams form a root communication between you and Nature and can break through overly linear modes of perception. This inborn faculty can be applied with practical intent to discover new responses to the challenges of our time.

Picture a vast sparkling web. Watch as one strand quivers when touched by a drop of rain. You'll then see the entire web come to life as the vibrating strand transmits its signal to the whole. Now imagine that this shimmering web is the whole of the cosmos.

Even within the limits of our modern imagination, we can stitch together what remains of the wild tongue with a genuine love for the world. It's then that the power of the deep imagination is initiated. The web starts to vibrate, and it shakes us from the trance of estrangement into what ecospiritual scholar Thomas Berry called "the dream of Earth."

Dream Logic & Creative Play

What is the shared language between Earth and Earthling? How can we be in conversation with the very matrix we're woven into?

The language of dreams speaks to something weirder than the modern mind is accustomed to. Dream logic sneaks past the rational gatekeepers that tell us what is possible and what is not. On a nightly basis we see that far more information can be compressed into a single image than our linear minds can immediately grasp.

The brief rituals and monthly vignettes of Dreamfruit's *Lunar Tales* are richly infused packets of meaning designed to activate the nonlinear mind, strengthen your ability to imagine generatively, and invite you to the enchanted "wishing well" aligned with astrological timing (as inspired by Jan Spiller's *New Moon Astrology*).

Dream logic unlocks "moon mind," a hidden intelligence that can be tapped for insight and guidance. Within the world of Dreamfruit, we engage these images to divine a path through the uncertainties of our

Earth-moment and guide us toward the regenerative future that our earthling hearts and Gaia herself long for.

As you explore the moons ahead, bear in mind the meta-story of our moment — the living Earth has been imperiled *and* our creative nature is rising up. Dreamfruit wants to awaken your creative nature because that part of you fulfills a unique role in the spiritual ecology of the world.

By definition, creativity brings new possibilities into being. What better time than now to cultivate a playful and curious mind, nimble enough to envision new patterns and pathways toward something better?

We each have our own ways of being with moon mind. Techniques and symbolic associations are as wildly diverse as we are. As you navigate the *Lunar Tales*, explore your own methods and make "Notes from the Field" that help you be with the story's mystery rather than force meaning from it. As you wend your way through the land of Dreamfruit, do what works for you, which may change over time. 🌿

Degree Symbols & the Sky Story

There exists among the wild children of Earth an ancient practice of attuning to the Great Circle and gathering messages from its many degrees. These messages are conveyed in images, dreams, and stories received by us through the deep imagination.

As we connect with the organic flow of natural time, shifting attention from the grid of the Gregorian calendar, we can begin to sense these stories and images at play.

The Dreamfruit journey is shaped by many modes of knowing. Aside from the languages of Nature, divination and dream, monthly themes are partly informed by the language of astrological degree symbols, specifically a system known as the Sabian symbols — a collection of 360 phrases recorded in 1925 by psychic Elsie Wheeler and astrologer Marc Edmund Jones, each corresponding to a degree of the zodiac.

This book features the original 1925 phrasing of each New Moon's Sabian symbol, listed underneath its correlating illustration.

Years of studying degree symbols have shown me their lunar resonance, which unmistakably echoes themes from daily life. Each New Moon starts its cycle at a different degree of the zodiac, bringing forth the energies of the specific Sabian symbol linked to that degree.

Viewing the year's story through these symbols reveals a dreamscape we can enter with lucidity and intention. Each lunar tale is carefully spellcrafted to tune you into the voice of the cosmos, flex your deep imagination, and elevate your creative nature.

All of creation is dreaming and transmitting to itself all the time. Throughout the ages, witches, herbalists, and dream-tenders have traversed the communication lines between nature and psyche. By way of a few magical technologies — dream, image, and story — we can rest our own bodies alongside the dreaming body of Earth and, if luck is with us, hear Her reverie. The world of Dreamfruit has these birthright magics at its core. 🌸

Themes of 2026

This year's journey finds us clearing the way for a new vision of life to emerge. Embedded within the narrative flow of each dream-story of 2026 is the spiral of reconnection — based on beloved teacher Joanna Macy's *Work that Reconnects* — reminding us moon by moon to choose radical gratitude, to honor our pain and love for this world, to sense our deep relatedness with all life, and to go forth in service to a flourishing world.

Winter: GOOD TIDINGS
Clearing / Oracle / Becoming

We begin in the time of the three Winter Moons. Here, we are doing some heavy lifting to clear a path for new growth. These moons speak of emerging possibilities and cause for hope, but not without a sizable investment of sweat and effort.

Part of the work is to practice listening to the soft, true voices in our midst. Glorious things may emerge from strange packages; only time and careful tending will tell. Let yourself dream a better future and then put your shoulder to the wheel.

Spring: OPENING EYES
Refraction / Exposure / Courtship

The three Moons of Spring feel flirty and playful, even as heavy spells begin to break. The sacred prankster emerges as the agent of the very awakening we need. As the world breaks into a mosaic of color and light, pick up a kaleidoscope lens to turn on your second, inner, set of eyes.

    During this season, we might be surprised by shifting attitudes, but this sets us free to express what our hearts truly yearn for. We'll need to admit when we feel let down, snap out of it, and then woo a more beautiful wishbird.

Summer: PATIENCE
Upkeep / Anticipation / Falling Awake

As Summer approaches, we prepare the nest for strange new life to arrive. We draw energy inward, tend and strengthen as we wait. We'll need to avoid getting lulled into a comfortable stupor as we explore a two-sided coin: the immanent new world seeking to be born, and the necessary pruning that makes room for life to grow.

The Summer months call us into a radical sort of drudgery, insisting that we remain vigilant around the mundane functions of life. We must learn when to step back, recharge, and develop ways to wait without losing focus.

Autumn: GUARDIANSHIP
Invigoration / Containment / Fruitful Protector

In the time of the Fall Moons, the preceding seasons of re-visioning and humble tending now leap into decisive action. In the demands of the hour, we conjure our greatest strengths and deepest reserves to defend a miracle. These months are our time to seek excellence, serve justice, and rise rooted in the protection of all life.

During this culminating season of the year, life enters the world in new and surprising ways. We awaken to new vitality, interrupt harm, and embrace the cycle of life, death, and rebirth.

Winter 2027: TURNING THE WHEEL
Renewal

Although we learn a great deal about ourselves and make potent advances this year, the lessons of 2026 require more than hope. We must act with our shared power for the benefit of all life. A new day dawns in the Thirteenth Moon. It may feel hard-won and incomplete, so placing clear protections around this shining life will give it the space needed to grow strong.

The Thirteenth Moon marks an ending and a beginning as the Wheel turns and a new solar year begins. The discoveries and challenges from the prior year don't go away; they enrich us with strength and wisdom as we step toward the adventure of the year to come.

Invocation . . .

In the land of Dreamfruit, you will come upon a long silver coastline with morning mists and a sea-gray sunrise. There you see a small trust of women in scarlet robes walking the early morning waterline.

Hear them sing as they step barefoot through the cold wet foam. They sing to the pebbles and bits of bone scattered like runes across the sand. They toss the song to and fro, each adding a verse to create a living record of the dawn and the changes the night has brought to shore.

Dreamfruit is a call and response, a form of echolocation. It is how we know who and where we are in relation to the times at hand. It is how we measure the changes and read the runes. It is an augury, moon by moon.

The maps of this land tell us that a great fire breathes in the South, and the Eastern dawn brings light from the mind of creation. The waters of this land are vast and deep and clearly situated to the West, flowing and lapping against the chthonic shores to the North, home of ancestors and our winter lodge where we go to dream through the long night.

In the heart of this land, the World Tree reaches deeply into both Earth and Sky, and so the map also requires above and below.

Bow to the four directions, and to the earth below and the sky above. Feel yourself held in the circle of the world. Now breathe.

As you consider the terrain of the coming year, the unfolding story with all of its knowns and unknowns, give yourself a picture of the world you most want to walk within. Consider the days and months ahead as a tiny but consequential sliver in the span of geologic time.

And so, here we are, gathered for the dawn of a new time. And we are stitching it fervently to the robes of Deep Time. A path appears, and we step through the gate together.

Clearing

{ F I R S T   M O O N }

December 19, 2025 – January 17, 2026

new: 12/19/25
29 sagittarius

full: 1/03/2026
14 cancer

"A fat boy mowing the lawn."

∼ 29 sagittarius ∼

IN THE DREAM OF THE CLEARING MOON, *we begin in our humble homes and in the streets of the cities. Yet we can feel the brecking as a sacred thing slips from the world.*

A mantra of remembering rises in our throats. We repeat truths from our journey. We sing of visioning caves, of great mists lifting, the stream guiding us to belonging.

Our skin quivers with memory of treebark, humming crystal, ancient water. In these moments, we bend to the bridge-tending work at hand, ensuring the path to Earthmind remains open.

And have we accepted the earthling bargain? And are we prepared for the sacred tasks ahead?

**By your hands, my love,
the way is sustained.**

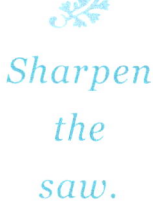

Sharpen

the

saw.

Clearing

As you begin 2026, take stock of current conditions and clear the path toward something new.

Tie your shoes, hydrate, and get moving. There's work to be done, and it's got your name written all over it. Keep up your end of the cosmic bargain.

Find dignity in stewardship. Some appearances are worth keeping up. Stretch your good-neighbor policy to include even the most basic gestures.

Give your emerging accountability a serious workout. Sober efforts will improve the view. Keep sight of your purpose and clear the path toward it.

Create a mantra to recall your earthling nature. Repeat daily.

1

Oracle

{ S E C O N D   M O O N }

January 18 – February 16, 2026

new: 1/18/26
29 capricorn

full: 2/01/26
14 leo

"A woman reading tea leaves."

~ 29 capricorn ~

IN THE DREAM OF THE ORACLE MOON, *we brew water and leaf in a ritual of conjuring. We gaze into the steam as if through enchanted glass.*

We see an egg, wings, new life flowing toward us. The world trembling with seas swallowing shorelines, forests gasping for air, our voices drowned by unshed tears.

The tea speaks in spirals and swirls, bringing a healing vision: the golden ratio threading through galaxy and fern frond alike. We read the conspiracy of mycelium and root, the gossip of wind in the branches, the truth-telling of stones.

Our voices open with love and grief. We rise as godsisters to the living world.

And do we speak what's true before us? And can we now be heard?

Yes. Believe the women.

Spill

the

tea.

Oracle

We are in the season of Good Tidings, so take notes and take comfort.

Neptune, spiritual ruler of the waters, dons his Warrior nature in Aries until 2039. Refer back to March-October 2025 for a hint at dreamy themes to come.

Your ally may be a charming teacup, a wise woman of prehistory such as Hypatia or Sosipatra of Pergamum, your favorite oracle deck, or divination technique of choice.

Capricorn themes for this month's wishcasting include self-discipline, future security, concrete achievement, and personal authority.

Is there a vision of life you are ready to lift up?

2

Becoming

{ T H I R D   M O O N }

February 17 – March 17, 2026

new: 2/17/26   full: 3/03/26
29 aquarius   13 virgo

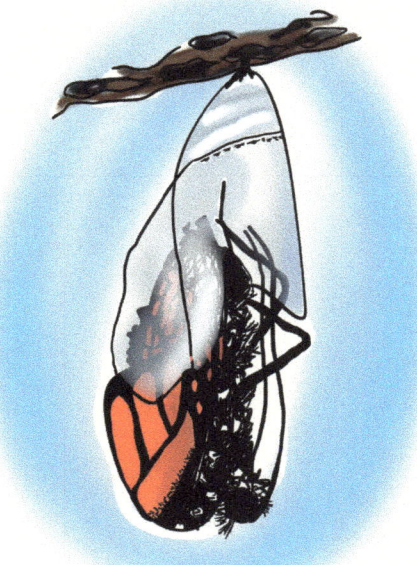

"Butterfly emerging from chrysalis."

~ 29 aquarius ~

*I*N THE DREAM OF THE BECOMING MOON,
rumors of a twiceborn, a changeling
slowly taking form, an egg, stages of
becoming. It is not an egg the oracle gave
us, but a bundle, tea leaves that now split
open like a cocoon.

The world's feverdreams persist
around us, systems cracking like dried
earth, but we no longer flinch at the sound.

Something crystallizes in our chests—
patterns coming into focus like wings of
stained glass. What was once a chrysalis is
now a flight path.

We stretch our gossamer strength
and feel a new hope unfurling within us,
brilliant and inevitable as sunrise.

And does the cocoon give way as life
pushes through?

Yes. It cannot be contained.

Remember

you can

fly.

3

Becoming

Maybe the fog is actually a conjuring mist for your crisp unfolding wings.

Eclipse season cracks open new possibilities while Saturn and Neptune create a zero point for astonishing life force to break through. The wonders you can imagine must be fed by follow-through.

A magical ally may be found in a good pair of scissors, future beings, elegant gadgets, or creatures never before dreamed.

This moon's Aquarian themes for wishmaking include innovation, long-range plans, friendships, and telling it like it is.

What strange angels do you see on the horizon?

3

Refraction

{ F O U R T H   M O O N }

March 18 – April 16, 2026

new: 3/18/26   full: 4/01/26

29 pisces   13 libra

"A prism."

~ 29 pisces ~

IN THE DREAM OF THE **REFRACTION MOON,** *the sun and moon shine through our newly dried wings to cast bright colors across the mossy stones.*

Even as the World of Forgetting flattens into two colors or three, we tilt our heads and soften our gaze until myriad colors shine through, drawing a hidden spectrum into focus.

A kaleidoscope of butterflies flutters between us and constellates into a sparkling rainbow bridge. Enfolding the vulnerable in our wondrous wings, we become a living prism, a sanctuary of passage.

And does a mandala bloom from the chaos? And are we both one and many?

Yes. Your multitudes form the bridge.

Embody
the spectrum.

4

Refraction

It's Spring! Closed mental attitudes quietly pop open as unseen helpers subtly clear the haze. Open an inner set of eyes to perceive fresh combinations and see what wants to thrive.

Your ally may show up as a pollinator, the Melissae bee priestesses, a suncatcher, or a Pink Floyd favorite.

Good Pisces themes for this month's wishing include imagination, healing, spirituality, and unity.

Saturn strikes up a conversation with Pluto to inform the months ahead. Feed structures that can survive powerful change, and release what is ready to compost back into Earth.

What can help you see it differently?

4

Exposure

{ F I F T H   M O O N }

April 17 – May 15, 2026

new: 4/17/26　　　　full: 5/01/26
28 aries　　　　　　12 scorpio

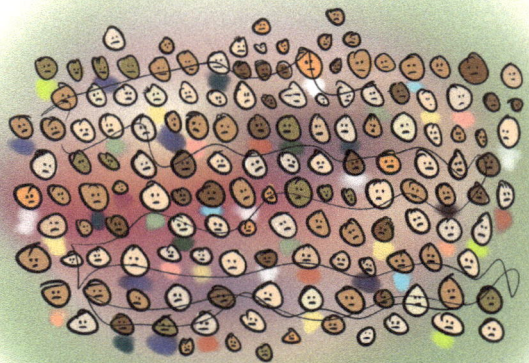

"A large disappointed audience."

~ 28 aries ~

IN THE DREAM OF THE EXPOSURE MOON, *a splendid tent rises through the forest canopy. With our creaturekin we flock from all directions, colors blazing. But the Mistress of Light has retreated to shadow, leaving hollow and listless performances to show in her place.*

Everyone can see the harsh light is a staged one, a mirage stealing life from the world. Our very colors drain until a weak beacon is all we can muster. But the nature sprites spot the danger and burst into a clever and bawdy dance.

Weakened but brave, we join them. With pounding hearts, we make an absurd but joyful noise and drive the loudmouths from the hall.

And does empire wither under the true light of Life?

Yes. The folly is the liberation.

*Flip
the script.*

Exposure

When the spectacle lets you down, check your toybox and see what playful spirits you can conjure. Hottest picks are connection and truth. This may call for walking away from an old favorite.

Uranus awakens the innovative mind through 2033 and meets up with Venus in a display of surprising beauty as they step into Gemini together April 25th.

You may find an ally in rainbow suspenders, a clear mirror, Baubo or the sprite who reigns over dawn, mirth, arts and revelry.

How does it look with the lights turned way up?

Themes to wish on for this Aries lunation include courage, beginnings, independence and self-expression.

5

Courtship

{SIXTH MOON}

May 16 – June 13, 2026

new: 5/16/26
26 taurus

full: 5/31/26
10 sagittarius

"A spaniard serenading his señorita."

~ 26 taurus ~

IN THE **D**REAM OF THE **C**OURTSHIP **M**OON, *we remember when the blessed Goddess walked among us and we laid petals on the path at Her feet. The Separation myth lost its charm long ago — knowing only how to lay claim, relying on conquest, not invitation.*

Now we must fortify what we love with beauty, sing the songs of remembering. Our pulse quickens like bird wings as we lay out our best offerings. We court the forests, the deep waters, the wide prairie, desert, tundra, and glade with tender attentions.

And are we courted in return by the wild itself? And can the holy landbond be restored?

Shine up your feathers, for you are the world loving herself.

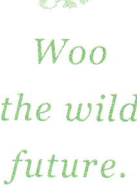

Woo

the wild

future.

6

Courtship

Pluto's retrograde calls each of us to reconsider what deep transformation can look like. It might be joyful. Create loving delights to set out as enticements to Gaia and her many children.

Practice consent and adoration as you seek your beloveds' attentions.

You may find an ally in the poets Mirabai or Sappho, an animal-familiar, songs of yearning, or a long-stemmed rose.

Natural and personal resources take a leading role in our thinking and planning. Intentions for the month ahead focus on Taurus themes of comfort, self-worth, patience, and pleasure.

How can you be an irresistible agent of a flourishing world?

6

Upkeep

{ S E V E N T H   M O O N }

June 14 – July 13, 2026

new: 6/14/26   full: 6/29/26
25 gemini   9 capricorn

"A man trimming palms."

∼ 25 gemini ∼

IN THE DREAM OF THE UPKEEP MOON, *we take up our place as Earth's beloveds, only to find that loudmouths have driven the caretaker from the grounds. Gardens are now unkempt, generations of care and knowledge lost.*

This Spirit of Place has been harmed and neglected. How could we possibly meet its needs?

We take up our shears. Our muscles remember ancestral work, shoulders satisfied in their tiredness. Small acts of care ripple through our muscles and through the web of life.

And are we humble in our efforts? And do young new shoots show their faces?

Yes. Steady tending protects the weave.

Practice the keeper's craft.

7

Upkeep

The dignity in simple tasks has never disappeared. Re-enchant the demands of the mundane.

The Full Moon heralds big energy shifts with some amount of fanfare. Patience can bring healing reward as Mercury begins its retrograde cycle and Chiron enters a slower pace in Taurus.

Allies may include your best pruning shears, a comic book or mixtape, a good broom, ancestor priestess Marie Leveau.

Wishcraft themes for this Gemini lunation include social connection, curiosity and learning, communication, and neighborly bonds.

When is it too tight? When is it too loose?

7

Anticipation

{ E I G H T H   M O O N }

July 14 – August 11, 2026
new: 7/14/26   full: 7/29/26
22 cancer   7 aquarius

"A woman awaiting a sailboat."

~ 22 cancer ~

IN THE DREAM OF THE ANTICIPATION MOON, *we feel our deep kinship breathing into and through the world. The distant waters are carrying something toward us. We know because in our quiet moments we hear it softly singing over the lake.*

The world of speed has gained instant results, and lost meaning in equal measure. But Time is a midwife to life itself, sovereign in her patience.

We make vigil as our breath slows to match the lapping shore. We are suspended in the Great Between as a dream takes shape, a child forms, a future gestates in its perfect time.

And does our love feed what we cannot see? And can we pray while we wait?

Yes. You are growing into a guardian of the possible.

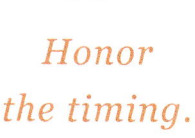

*Honor
the timing.*

8

Anticipation

Set your sights on new shores, and trust you will be carried across the waters.

Look up! Great constellations are formed from clusters of tiny lights. Venus traveling through Virgo asks us to tend small things in order to make a great thing beautiful.

Things start to sizzle as Uranus forms early aspects, hinting at the themes of its 8-year tour through Gemini.

At this Cancer new moon consider wish-making around themes of nourishment, motherhood, protection, and home.

Seek your magical ally in a feathered nest, a manger, binoculars and sunscreen.

Can you wait for an invisible thing to come around? How will you know?

8

Falling Awake

{ N I N T H   M O O N }

August 12 – September 9, 2026

new: 8/12/26   full: 8/27/26
21 leo   5 pisces

"Chickens intoxicated."

~21 leo~

IN THE DREAM OF THE FALLING AWAKE, *the world is alight with the twinkle-and-wink antics of raven, fox, imp and wind. We grow evermore enchanted with the moon on the water.*

The World of Forgetting once lulled us from this treasure, its tricks and mimics nearly sweeping us away. Yet we are now steadied by our earth-bond.

Our wildkin prance around us in a gentle circle, drawing us to the place of the wild honey. The ordinary dissolves into kaleidoscope shards as rivers of color flow through our eyes.

And does the web of kinship shimmer into view?

Yes. The lens can be both wild and wide.

Add
a pinch
of salt.

9

Falling Awake

Choose Leo wishing themes for this new moon: creativity, generosity, playfulness, honor, and pride.

Your magical ally will more likely appear in micro-doses than in heroic ones. Perhaps a cold water plunge, a hammock, and a digital fast are in order.

Eclipse season is here. Enjoy unusual diversions and reach beyond what you believe limits you. Aim high but try to grow at a pace that your whole self can keep up with.

As Venus opposes Neptune, boundaries get melty. Let the wild creative mind out to play but don't lose sight of your true vow.

When is it time to snap out of it? And how do you?

9

Invigoration

{ T E N T H   M O O N }

September 10 – October 9, 2026

new: 9/10/26
19 virgo

full: 9/26/26
4 aries

"A swimming race."

~ 19 virgo ~

IN THE DREAM OF THE **INVIGORATION MOON,** *it is said that waters churned by sprites bestows a healing boon, but those once sparkling waters have grown stagnant and rank.*

Beaver, muskrat and dragonfly all join us along the banks. The opposite shore has been silent for so long. Then out of the dark, the yodeling luminous loon sends its wail across the waters. Its peal sets us into motion, toward the call of life.

We leap into the cool waters just as a lively frolic of nixies rises to meet us, and so we have been blessed.

And are we crackling with life? And does a great sound erupt from our throats?

Yes. For there are so many hurting.

Trouble

the

waters.

Invigoration

Virgo season invites your wish-making around themes of precision, service, organization, and work.

Your magical ally may appear as endurance swimmer Diana Nyad, a pod of dolphins or mermaids, the quickening spark, a pool noodle, a thoughtful conversation, a stopwatch.

The three moons of Fall bring us into the season of Guardianship. Look back at July and August of 2025 for echoes of this month's Grand Air Trine.

What ignites your inner champion?

This is a time to train for victory and act fiercely on behalf of all life.

10

Containment

{ E L E V E N T H   M O O N }

October 10 – November 7, 2026

new: 10/10/26   full: 10/25/26
18 libra   3 taurus

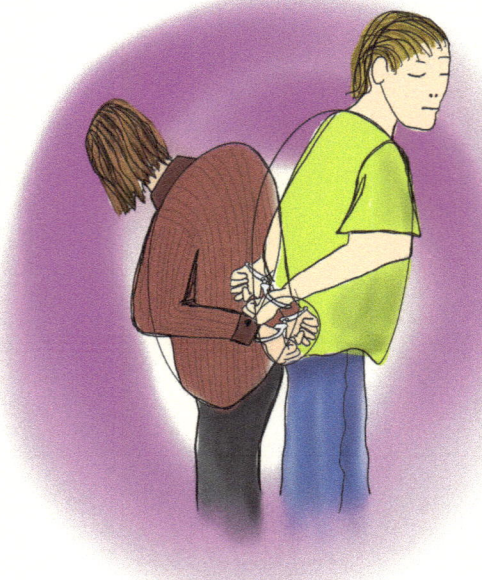

"Two men placed under arrest."

~ 18 libra ~

IN THE DREAM OF THE CONTAINMENT MOON, *we rise in glory from the lake's glittering shore, buoyed by the singing waters.*

But the loudmouths have grown mired in their own mud bog, grasping at our ankles to save themselves.

We waterlings, wise ones, and earth-rooted warriors deftly build a swirl of power. With a great roar, our roots reach deep below as we spread our stained glass wings. Those wings that once served as sanctuary now braid like breathing branches into a fiercely dancing ring.

"By the magic of three by three, we bind you Division and Greed from harming others and from harming thee."

And does Justice encircle us? As shelter and as storm?

Yes. The immovable can be moved.

Make
it stop.

Containment

With this new moon, Libran themes to carry to the wishing well include justice, harmony, diplomacy, partnerships and karma.

Magical allies could appear as toolkits of any sort, ankle weights, a set of scales, mighty ancestor Ruth Bader Ginsburg, the word "no."

Venus traces her steps back into Libra's halls of Beauty and Truth. All hands on deck. Cast a strengthening spell for Lady Justice, and another one to sequester the harmful ways.

Are there harms to be grieved? Amends to be made?

Rilke says, "This is how we grow: by being defeated, decisively, by constantly greater beings."

11

Fruitful Protector

{ T W E L F T H   M O O N }

November 8 – December 7, 2026

new: 11/08/26   full: 11/24/26
17 scorpio   3 gemini

"A woman the father of her own child."

~ 17 scorpio ~

IN THE **DREAM OF THE FRUITFUL PROTECTOR,** *what the oracle foretold in the Second Moon now comes to pass — a rising creative power indistinguishable from miracles. This quicksilver was almost stolen and chained, but now we feel the quickening in our core.*

We have been shaping a wild new life, conjuring a magical child from clay and salt, water and wind. We sing ancient powersongs as Life Force pours through us and into the world.

From quiet intent to incubation to churned waters to this moment of impossible birth, the cycle renews itself.

And are we all at once — Sacred Father, Great Mother, and the One newly emerged?

Yes. You are stronger than you think.

Open

the

gate.

Fruitful Protector

Explore Scorpio themes in your lunar wish-making, including emotional honesty, letting go, regeneration, debt, and personal power.

A magical ally may be waiting in your very own sacred body, the whiptail lizard who reproduces through gynogenesis, or a moon-centered calendar.

Make an offering to the great goddess Isis, the Blessed Virgin, the Sacred Hag, She who appears in many guises. Chant the endless names of the Great Mother to invoke a powerful force of creation.

Is there something you're creating no matter what?

12

Renewal

{ T H I R T E E N T H   M O O N }

December 8, 2026 – January 6, 2027

new: 12/08/26
17 sagittarius

full: 12/23/26
3 cancer

"An Easter sunrise service."

~ 17 sagittarius ~

IN THE DREAM OF THE RENEWAL MOON, *one by one our travelkin and wild familiars appear in the morning mist, in a grove of newly sprouted saplings.*

We tell the story of Business as Usual and its long resistance to the cycle of life and death. But every ending contains the seeds of its own return. Here, we are learning to let go in order to renew.

We weave between the trees in a dance of Great Turning, met by the morning star, the four winds, and the guardian of the woods. Today we can see. On this day wash'd new.

And do we gather like children? To welcome life back into the world?

**By the dawn, my love,
let us raise you up.**

Assemble

the

multitudes.

13

Renewal

The year is winding down, and you may want to transition into your new Dreamfruit 2027.

But before you go, take some time to review all that you've discovered on your journey. Reflect on your Notes from the Field to cull any medicine meant for you.

When you are ready, turn to Closing the Gate for a guided meditation to reveal and gather your personal fruits for the year.

Your notions of healing might surprise you. Old wounds are met with spontaneous remission.

What shining world can you imagine?

13

Closing the Gate

Thank you for traveling through the landscape of Dreamfruit 2026. The year is closing as our Sun rounds the corner to begin a new solar cycle. Take a moment to look back on your path and gather the fruits of your journey to carry into the year ahead . . .

*. . . **We return to the misty shoreline** where the scarlet-robed women have been listening all year. They have been here with their bare feet tracing patterns in the sand, translating your steps into shape and song. Step closer and see the design their path makes in the cool damp sand.*

One by one, they gather in circle around you. Thirteen of them side by side.

They see you. They have heard you crying and laughing as the moons grew and waned. They have divined wisps of your dreams as through a sea glass window. They each hold a verse to share about your journey, that only you can hear. If you're willing, ask them a question and let their answer be written across the threshold of the gate. 🌸

WHAT FRUITS ARE WAITING
FOR YOU AT THE GATE?

ABOUT THE AUTHOR

Poet, witch, and joyful earthling, Elizabeth Russell has apprenticed herself to the voice of nature for most of her life. Her work inspires us to reconnect with the intelligence of the living Earth by awakening our birthright powers of deep imagination.

With the Dreamfruit series, she has created an enchanted world that brings the Great Turning to life in our imagination and daily lives.

Elizabeth lives in the beautiful Pacific Northwest, where she feeds the birds and leads visionary experiments to inspire radical engagement with the living cosmos.

Themes from *Lunar Tales for Earthlings* are expanded upon in monthly mixtapes, monthly storytelling videos, and in the *Dreamfruit Journal Magic for Earthlings* — available at www. Dreamfruit.world. ✿

Bonus
Journal
Art
Pages

The following removable pages are designed
for integrated play with the *Dreamfruit
Journal Magic for Earthlings.*

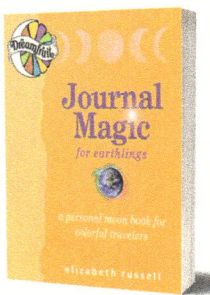

With each lunar cycle, cut out the associated
sheet to paste into the space provided in
your personal moon book as a springboard
into the imaginal realm.

Don't have the journal?
You can get one at *www.Dreamfruit.world*,
or simply cut out the cards moon by moon
for personal altar work.

The phrases correspond to the astrological degree
symbol for each new moon of the year (Sabian system).

Art by Beth Lorio

Clearing

{ F I R S T   M O O N }

December 19, 2025 – January 17, 2026

new: 12/19/25   full: 1/03/2026
29 sagittarius   14 cancer

"A fat boy mowing the lawn."

~ 29 sagittarius ~

Sharpen

the

saw.

Oracle

{ S E C O N D   M O O N }

January 18 – February 16, 2026

new: 1/18/26   full: 2/01/26
29 capricorn   14 leo

"A woman reading tea leaves."

~ 29 capricorn ~

*Spill
the
tea.*

Sabian symbol illustration by Beth Lorio.

www.Dreamfruit.world

Becoming

{ T H I R D   M O O N }

February 17 – March 17, 2026

new: 2/17/26　　　　full: 3/03/26
29 aquarius　　　　13 virgo

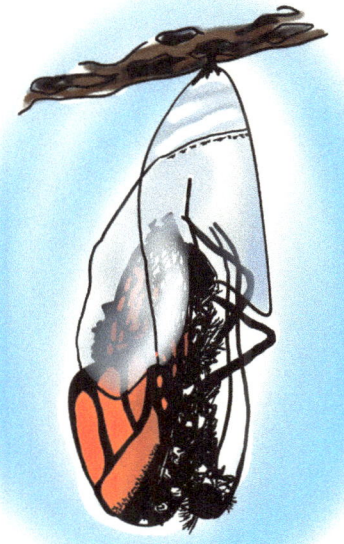

"Butterfly emerging from chrysalis."

~ 29 aquarius ~

Remember
you can
fly.

Sabian symbol illustration by Beth Lorio.

www.Dreamfruit.world

Refraction

{ F O U R T H   M O O N }

March 18 – April 16, 2026

new: 3/18/26   full: 4/01/26
29 pisces   13 libra

"A prism."

∼ 29 pisces ∼

Embody

the

spectrum.

Sabian symbol illustration by Beth Lorio.

www.Dreamfruit.world

Exposure

{ F I F T H   M O O N }

April 17 – May 15, 2026

new: 4/17/26　　　　full: 5/01/26
28 aries　　　　　　12 scorpio

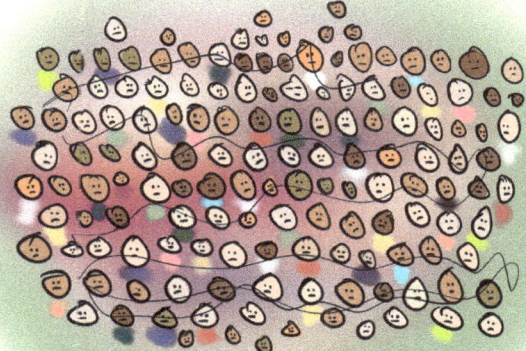

"A large disappointed audience."

~ 28 aries ~

*Flip
the
script.*

Sabian symbol illustration by Beth Lorio.

www.Dreamfruit.world

Courtship

{ SIXTH MOON }

May 16 – June 13, 2026

new: 5/16/26   full: 5/31/26
26 taurus   10 sagittarius

"A spaniard serenading his señorita."

~ 26 taurus ~

Woo
the wild
future.

Sabian symbol illustration by Beth Lorio.

www.Dreamfruit.world

Upkeep

{ S E V E N T H   M O O N }

June 14 – July 13, 2026

new: 6/14/26
25 gemini

full: 6/29/26
9 capricorn

"A man trimming palms."

∼ 25 gemini ∼

Practice
the keeper's
craft.

Anticipation

{ E I G H T H M O O N }

July 14 – August 11, 2026

new: 7/14/26
22 cancer

full: 7/29/26
7 aquarius

"A woman awaiting a sailboat."

~ 22 cancer ~

Honor
the
timing.

Falling Awake

{ N I N T H   M O O N }

August 12 – September 9, 2026
new: 8/12/26   full: 8/27/26
21 leo   5 pisces

"Chickens intoxicated."

~21 leo~

Add
a pinch
of salt.

Invigoration

{ T E N T H   M O O N }

September 10 – October 9, 2026

new: 9/10/26   full: 9/26/26
19 virgo   4 aries

"A swimming race."

~ 19 virgo ~

Trouble
the
waters.

Sabian symbol illustration by Beth Lorio.

www.Dreamfruit.world

Containment

{ E L E V E N T H   M O O N }

October 10 – November 7, 2026

new: 10/10/26   full: 10/25/26
18 libra   3 taurus

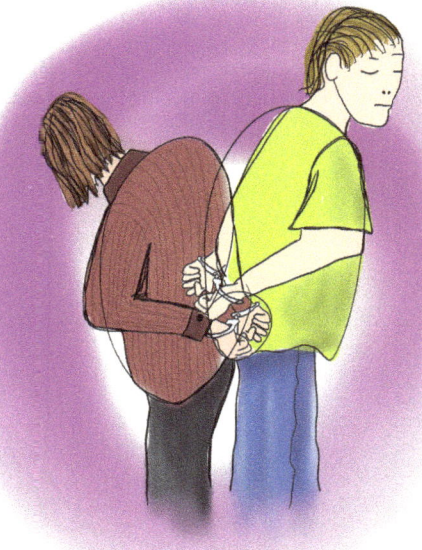

"Two men placed under arrest."

~ 18 libra ~

Make

it

stop.

Sabian symbol illustration by Beth Lorio.

www.Dreamfruit.world

Fruitful Protector

{ T W E L F T H M O O N }

November 8 – December 7, 2026

new: 11/08/26
17 scorpio

full: 11/24/26
3 gemini

"A woman the father of her own child."

~ 17 scorpio ~

Open

the

gate.

Sabian symbol illustration by Beth Lorio.

www.Dreamfruit.world

Renewal

{ T H I R T E E N T H   M O O N }

December 8, 2026 – January 6, 2027

new: 12/08/26   full: 12/23/26
17 sagittarius   3 cancer

"An Easter sunrise service."

~ 17 sagittarius ~

Assemble
the
multitudes.

.

Sabian symbol illustration by Beth Lorio.

www.Dreamfruit.world

www.ingramcontent.com/pod-product-compliance
Lightning Source LLC
Chambersburg PA
CBHW051652120626
46551CB00015B/2328